MW01153773

FACTORY ROBOTS

BY ELIZABETH NOLL

Blastoff! Discovery launches
a new mission: reading to learn.
Filled with facts and features,
each book offers you an exciting
new world to explore!

This edition first published in 2018 by Bellwether Media, Inc.

No part of this publication may be reproduced in whole or in
part without written permission of the publisher.
For information regarding permission, write to Bellwether
Media, Inc., Attention: Permissions Department,
5357 Penn Avenue South, Minneapolis, MN 55419.

Library of Congress Cataloging-in-Publication Data

Names: Noll, Elizabeth, author.
Title: Factory Robots / by Elizabeth Noll.
Description: Minneapolis, MN : Bellwether Media, Inc., [2018]
    | Series: Blastoff! Discovery. World of Robots | Audience:
    Ages 7-13. | Includes bibliographical references and index.
Identifiers: LCCN 2016053593 (print) | LCCN 2016055669
    (ebook) | ISBN 9781626176874 (hardcover : alk. paper)
    | ISBN 9781681034171 (ebook)
    | ISBN 9781618912909 (paperback : alk. paper)
Subjects: LCSH: Robots, Industrial—Juvenile literature. |
    Robotics—Juvenile literature.
Classification: LCC TS191.8 .N65 2018 (print) | LCC TS191.8
    (ebook) | DDC 670.42/72—dc23
LC record available at https://lccn.loc.gov/2016053593

Editor: Christina Leaf   Designer: Jon Eppard

Printed in the United States of America, North Mankato, MN.

TABLE OF CONTENTS

FACTORY ROBOT AT WORK!

One day, Eli and Odell found a surprise at work. It was a red robot. It was working on their assembly line. The boss introduced the robot as Baxter. It was a new member of the team.

Baxter had big arms and a square face. Its metal arms picked up gears. Then it put each gear carefully into a box. Odell and Eli were worried. It worked twice as fast as either of them!

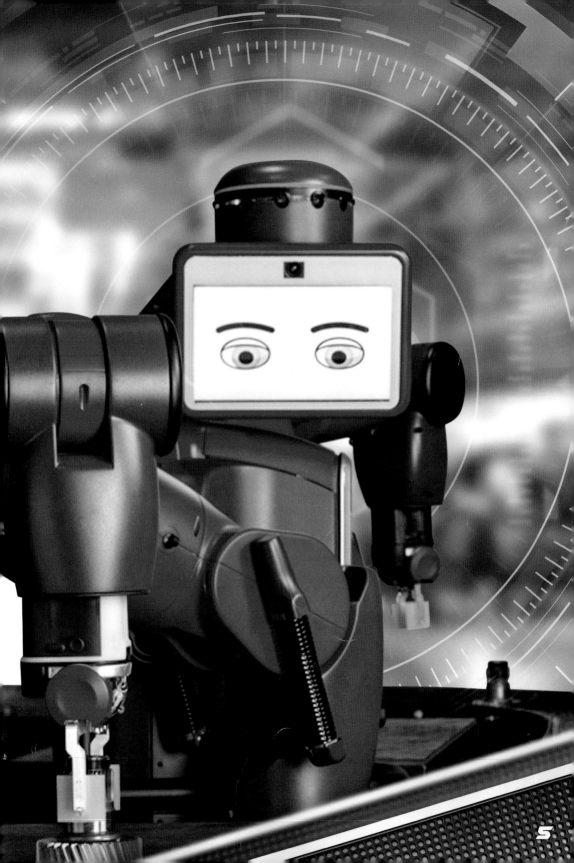

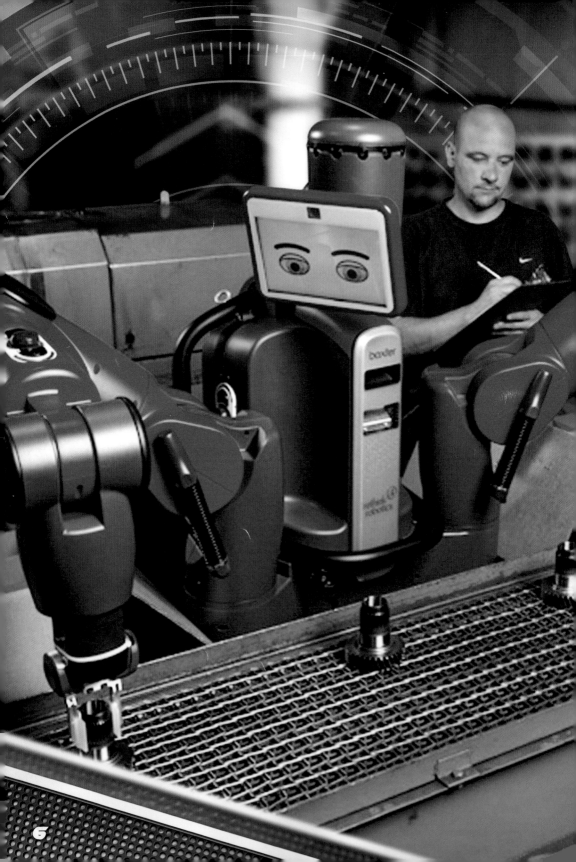

The boss assured them that Baxter was not there to replace anybody. It was there to help them with rush orders. They had to ship one hundred boxes of gears that morning and could use the extra help.

Everybody worked as fast as they could. Baxter's arms moved without stopping. With five minutes to spare, they packed the last box. They all breathed a sigh of relief. Maybe this new robot was not so bad after all!

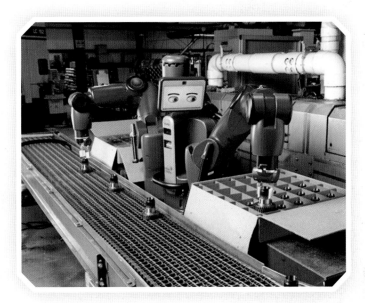

RUN, ROBOTS, RUN!

On September 21, 2016, Adidas released the Futurecraft M.F.G. This was the first shoe made in the company's robot-run factory in Germany.

WHAT ARE FACTORY ROBOTS?

Working in a factory can be dangerous. Toxic chemicals or sheets of hot metal might be needed to make products like cars or computers. A factory can also be boring. Assembly lines require the same simple action again and again.

Factory robots are here to help! Some do jobs that are too difficult or dangerous for humans. Others take over repetitive tasks. They can work faster than humans and do not get tired or bored.

robot arm welding elevator parts

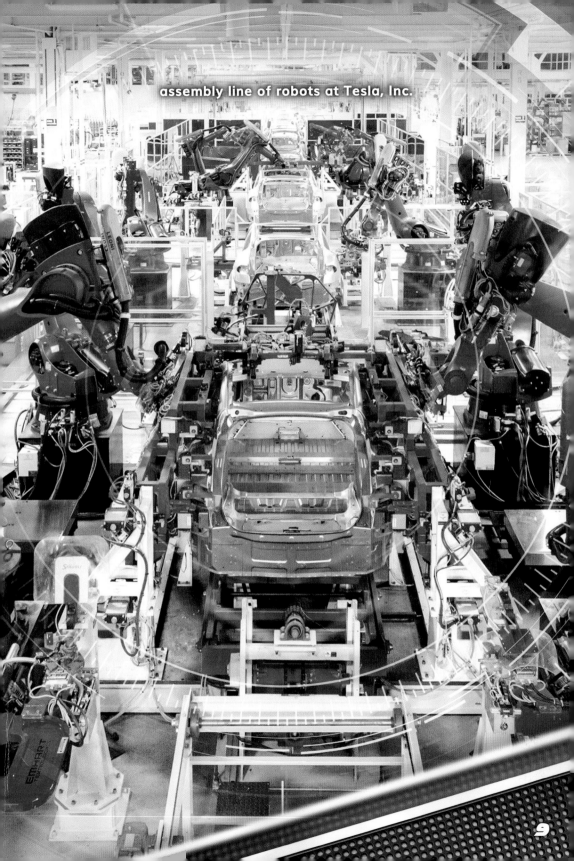

assembly line of robots at Tesla, Inc.

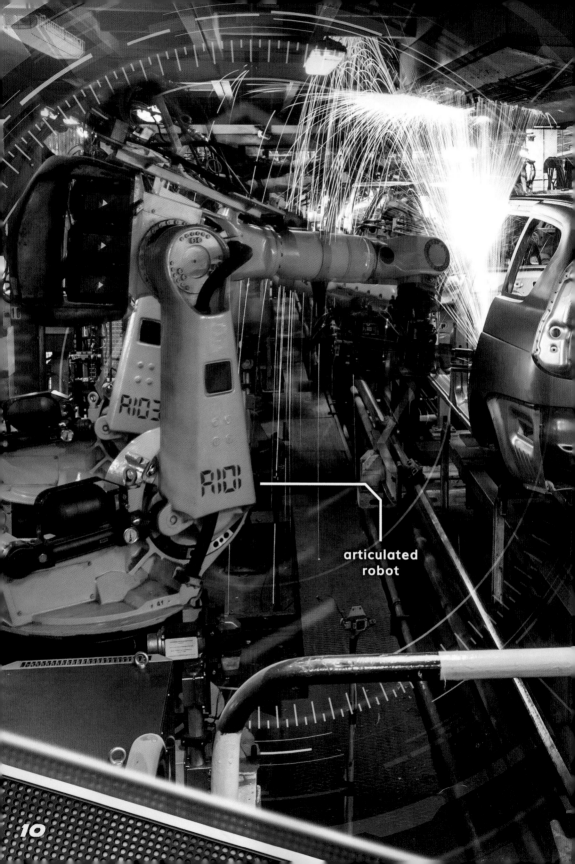

articulated
robot

Most factory robots do not look human. They look like giant steel arms. At the end of each arm is a tool called an **end effector**. This tool can take different forms depending on what is needed for the task.

There are three main types of factory robots. Each type moves its arm in a different way.

An **articulated** robot has several joints that rotate. This type of robot does a lot of **welding**, spray painting, metal cutting, and assembly. Many help make cars.

gripper end effector

welding head end effector

Linear robots are also called Cartesian robots. They move along three straight **axes** that are **perpendicular** to one another. Two axes move horizontally and one moves vertically. Linear

linear robot

robots are often used for moving heavy loads or assembling products.

SCARA robots are the most common factory robot. They move at 4 different points, so they are **precise** but also have a flexible range of motion. Their motion is mainly horizontal. SCARA robots are very good at **pick and place**.

MOTION OF THREE MAIN TYPES
OF FACTORY ROBOTS

articulated robot

linear robot

SCARA robot

⚠ 警告

ロボットの稼働部に手
を近づけないでくださ
い。
はさんでケガをするお
それがあります。

TOSHIBA MACHINE

SCARA robot

NOT FOR MAILING

Each robot has a certain
amount of space it can
work within. This is called
a work envelope.

THE DEVELOPMENT OF FACTORY ROBOTS

In 1961, United States company General Motors (GM) installed Unimate, the very first factory robot. The robot weighed 4,000 pounds (1,814 kilograms). It did work that was dangerous for humans.

By 1969, GM had an assembly line of Unimate robots to weld car bodies in one of its factories. That same year, a company called Kawasaki produced the first Unimate robot in Japan.

GM assembly line, 1970

Soon, other factory robots started appearing. In 1969, a Norwegian factory began using a robot for spray painting. Then in 1973, the first six-axis robot appeared. It had a larger range of motion for even more tasks.

Unimate 2000B
(1979)

Unimate robots and other early factory robots were huge, expensive, and dangerous. They were not programmed to stop or even notice if a human was nearby. For that reason, most were behind large, protective cages.

But over time, factory robots became smaller and cheaper. This is because computers got smaller and cheaper.

Computers are the "brains" of robots. Over the last few decades, computers have shrunk from room-sized to palm-sized. They have also become much more advanced. Now, more powerful computers can fit into much smaller robots.

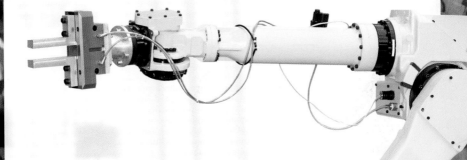

BIG BUCKS

Robots can be very expensive. Some cost more than $100,000!

Because they are smaller, factory robots are also less dangerous than they used to be. Some of them are much lighter than factory robots were decades ago. They can be made out of plastic or vinyl instead of big chunks of metal.

Some robots are collaborative. This means they can safely work next to humans. They have vision and touch sensors so they know where people are and can avoid crashes. If a human steps into their path, they stop.

collaborative robot

ROBOT GARGANTUA

More than 20 years before Unimate, a man named Griffith P. Taylor invented an industrial robot. It could stack wooden blocks. This robot never worked in a factory, however. In fact, most people never even heard about it.

FACTORY ROBOT PROFILE: UNIMATE

The very first robot to work in a factory was named Unimate. Unimate stacked hot metal and did other work that was dangerous for humans. It also built cars twice as fast as humans could.

Soon, companies all over the world decided to use Unimate robots. Unimate's robotic arms were fast and reliable. They could handle parts that weighed hundreds of pounds. Today, this kind of robotic arm is one of the most common factory robots!

Name:	Unimate
Developer:	Joseph Engelberger and George Devol
Release Date:	1961
Functions:	welding, metal transport
Size:	5.3 feet (1.6 meters) tall; 4 feet (1.2 meters) wide; 5 feet (1.5 meters) deep

A NOVEL IDEA

The idea for Unimate came from science fiction books. Joseph Engelberger loved Isaac Asimov's books about robots and talked with inventor George Devol about creating a robot. Three years later, Unimate was born.

FACTORY ROBOT PROFILE:
SCARA

In 1978, Japanese professor Hiroshi Makino invented the SCARA robot. This robot has a four-axis motion. That means it moves at four different points.

SCARA robots are perfect for many factory jobs. They are especially good at moving small parts very quickly. One expert says they can handle objects the size of a piece of dust! The SCARA is in the Robot Hall of Fame for its role in creating small electronics, like cell phones and tablets.

MEDICAL HELP

SCARA robots are very good at drilling holes for hip and knee surgery.

Name:	Selective Compliance Assembly Robot Arm
Nickname:	SCARA
Developer:	Professor Hiroshi Makino
Release Date:	1978
Functions:	pick up and move objects, electronics assembly
Size:	varies; from 4.7 inches (12 centimeters) to 59 inches (150 centimeters) arm length

SCARA robot assembling circuit boards

FACTORY ROBOT PROFILE:
BAXTER

Most factory robots look like machines. But Baxter's creator, former MIT professor Rodney Brooks, wanted his collaborative robot to look human. He even gave Baxter a computer-screen "face" that can show expressions. These expressions show humans what Baxter is doing. One shows it is learning. Another appears when it is confused.

It is easy to show Baxter what to do next. A worker does not need to know how to write code to teach it a task. Baxter learns by a human moving its arms through the tasks.

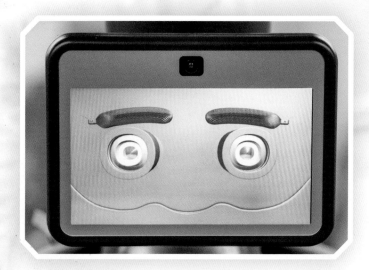

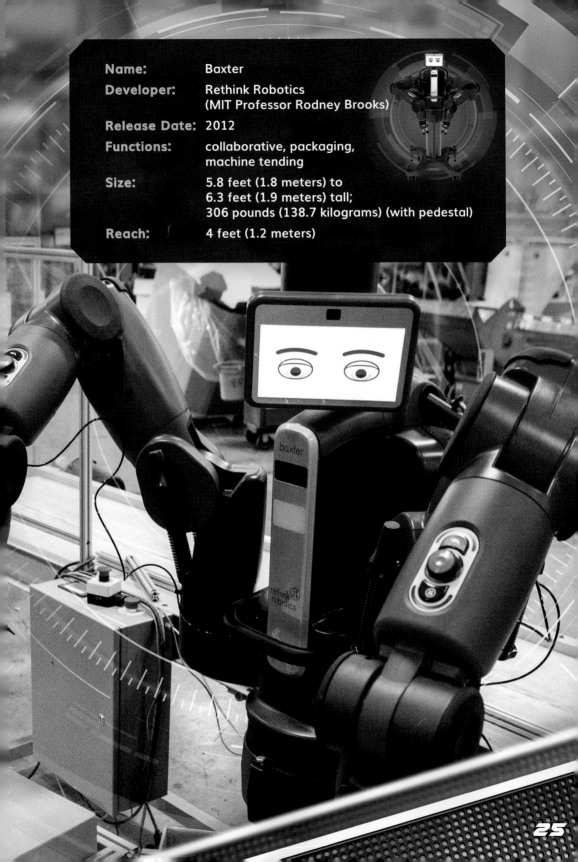

Name:	Baxter
Developer:	Rethink Robotics (MIT Professor Rodney Brooks)
Release Date:	2012
Functions:	collaborative, packaging, machine tending
Size:	5.8 feet (1.8 meters) to 6.3 feet (1.9 meters) tall; 306 pounds (138.7 kilograms) (with pedestal)
Reach:	4 feet (1.2 meters)

FACTORY ROBOT PROFILE:
YUMI

A company called ABB Robotics introduced YuMi in 2015. YuMi stands for you and me. It was created to work next to humans and along with them. Many factory robots are so large and heavy that they could hurt a human if something went wrong. But YuMi is human-sized and covered with soft padding.

YuMi easily learns new actions. A human worker simply moves YuMi's arms through the necessary steps to program it.

programming YuMi

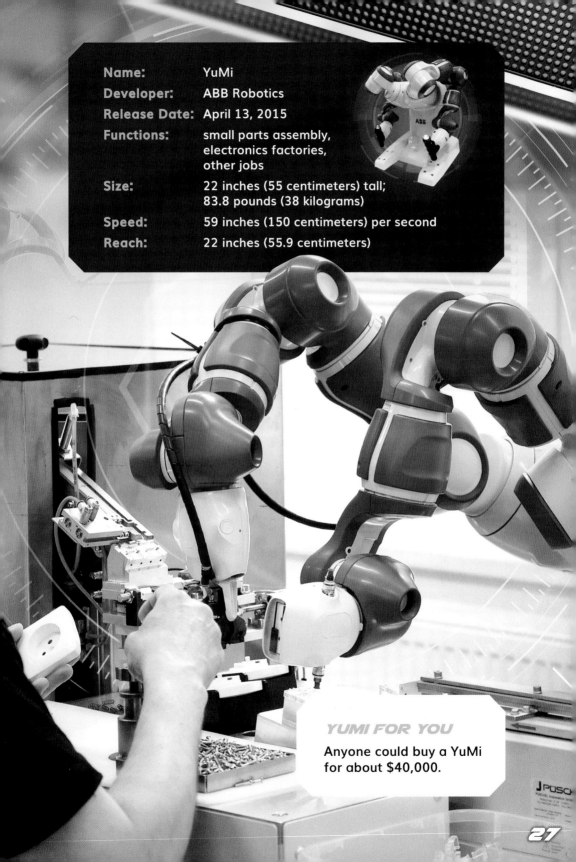

Name:	YuMi
Developer:	ABB Robotics
Release Date:	April 13, 2015
Functions:	small parts assembly, electronics factories, other jobs
Size:	22 inches (55 centimeters) tall; 83.8 pounds (38 kilograms)
Speed:	59 inches (150 centimeters) per second
Reach:	22 inches (55.9 centimeters)

YUMI FOR YOU

Anyone could buy a YuMi for about $40,000.

THE FUTURE OF FACTORY ROBOTS

Factory robots started out making cars, but now they do many things. They can pack cookies in boxes, build washing machines, test Xboxes, and do thousands of other tasks.

The number of robots built and bought each year keeps going up. Robots can help humans do things we never imagined. They can take over difficult or impossible tasks and free up humans to do new, more creative jobs. Who knows how far robots will take us!

robots packaging chocolates

robot assembling a
washing machine

GLOSSARY

articulated—connected by one or more joints

assembly line—an arrangement of workers or machines where work passes from one to the next until a product is put together

axes—directions used to specify robot motion

collaborative—able to work together with humans

end effector—a special tool at the end of a robot arm

perpendicular—at right angles

pick and place—the action of picking up one object and putting it somewhere else

precise—exact

repetitive—something that is repeated

sensors—devices that respond to light, pressure, sound, or other physical changes

welding—using heat to fasten pieces of metal together

TO LEARN MORE

AT THE LIBRARY

Ceceri, Kathy. *Robotics: Discover the Science and Technology of the Future with 20 Projects.* White River Junction, Vt.: Nomad Press, 2012.

Mara, Wil. *Robotics: From Concept to Consumer.* New York, N.Y.: Children's Press, 2015.

Ventura, Marne. *The 12 Biggest Breakthroughs in Robot Technology.* North Mankato, Minn.: 12-Story Library, 2015.

ON THE WEB

Learning more about factory robots is as easy as 1, 2, 3.

1. Go to www.factsurfer.com.

2. Enter "factory robots" into the search box.

3. Click the "Surf" button and you will see a list of related web sites.

With factsurfer.com, finding more information is just a click away.

INDEX

The images in this book are reproduced through the courtesy of: Nataliya Hora, front cover; SIPA USA/ Rethink Robotics via Sipa USA/ Newscom, pp. 4, 4-5, 6-7, 7, 25 (top); Si Wei - Imaginechina, p. 8; The Washington Post/ Contributor/ Getty Images, p. 9; Andrei Kholmov, pp. 10-11; S. Bonaime, p. 11 (top); Alan Bauman, p. 11 (bottom); Juan Martinez, pp. 12 (top), 17 (inset); Nicolas Primola, p. 12 (bottom); Aflo Co. Ltd./ Alamy Stock Photo, pp. 12-13, 23 (top), 27 (top); Library of Congress/ Handout/ Getty Images, p. 14; Science and Society, pp. 14-15, 21 (top); Cultura Limited, pp. 16-17; CTK/ Alamy Stock Photo, pp. 18, 26-27; Juice Images, pp. 18-19; Mark Andrews, p. 20; The Henry Ford Website, pp. 20-21; Prisma by Dukas Presseagentur GmbH/ Alamy Stock Photo, p. 22; Prisma, pp. 22-23; James Gourley/ ZUMA Press, p. 24; Kristoffer Tripplaar/ Alamy Stock Photo, pp. 24-25; dpa picture alliance/ Alamy Stock Photo, p. 26; Bloomberg/ Contributor/ Getty Images, p. 28; Andreas Rentz/ Staff/ Getty Images, pp. 28-29.